T0114321

Words
of
Encouragement
"Words that flow from the heart"

By: Centwane Daniel

authorHOUSE®

AuthorHouse™
1663 Liberty Drive
Bloomington, IN 47403
www.authorhouse.com
Phone: 1-800-839-8640

First published by AuthorHouse 10/13/2009

ISBN: 978-1-4490-2876-3 (sc)

Printed in the United States of America
Bloomington, Indiana

This book is printed on acid-free paper.

Contents

ACKNOWLEDGEMENTS

First I want to acknowledge my lovely wife for always being there for me, and believing in me, she mean a whole lot to me. My mother for raising me up right, and always being a good mother. Pastor Paul Thomas, I thank God for placing me up under your ministry at "Prayer and Praise" me and my wife have grown tremendously there. To a special man that I know I can call a FRIEND, none other than Frank Bussey, I thank God for placing you in my life, words from you helped me out a whole lot!!!! Thank you all so much and I love you dearly!

Dedication

To a special woman,
Who always stuck by my side.
So beautiful to me ,
A bloomed rose to my eyes.

Like the sun rays on the ocean,
She sparkles up my day.
I think of a beautiful angel ,
Every time I see her face.

A dream come true,
I know she was heaven sent.
Dressed in and earthly body,
"My" earth angel to you I present!!!

Salvation

"That if you confess with your mouth the Lord Jesus and believe in your heart that God has raised Him from the dead, you will be saved."
Romans10:9 NKJV

Gift of salvation

I believed in my heart,
Confessed on bended knee.
You gave me a gift,
And it came to me free.

You opened my eyes,
From the sins of my nature.
Scales fell as tears,
By the power of my maker.

Now I can shout feely,
My soul has been delivered.
Sins are in the sea of the forgetfulness,
By God, who is a great forgiver!

A loving God,
Since the beginning of creation.
I received freely,
the gift of Salvation!!

Create me in your image &likeness!

Lord keep me,
Covered under your blood.
Anoint me in your truth,
Empower and establish me by your word.

Deliver me where,
I am wretched and poor.
Bury me in your word,

Like the sand under the ocean's floor.

Crown me in your,
love and in your righteousness.
Let your glory shine through me,
Create me in your image and likeness!

Commit My Life

I confess with my mouth,
That you are Lord.
The ark of Jesus Christ,
I get aboard.

Nothing good lies,
In this world of sin.
Wash me white as snow,
May the spirit of Christ dwell within.

Create in me Lord,
A clean heart.
Confession of you Lord,
Gives me a clean start.

I present my body to you,
A living sacrifice.
For you Lord are holy,
In your hands I commit my life!

LOVE

"And though I have the gift of prophecy, and understand all mysteries and all knowledge, and though I have all faith, so that I could remove mountains, but have not love, I am nothing"
1Corinthians 13:2 NKJV

Love

Love is sincere, love builds
 through time.
Love is meekness, love is caring,
Love is longsuffering, love is forbearing,
Love will take a relationship, miles a long way,
Even in hard times love will cause you to stay.
Love will help you to look on the inner man,
If there's a difference between two, you will still
be a friend.
You'll stick together, no matter the storm.
Because through love the both of you were nicely
joined.
Love, is one of the most beautiful things in the
world.
There's nothing more beautiful, not even black
shiny pearls.
Where would we be, if love wasn't in the air?
That's something we'll never know, without love ,
life just want be fair!

What is Love

What is love,
If you do not have a mate?
What is love,
If you are a person of hate?

What is love,
If there's no lending of a helping hand?
What is love,
If there's not a caring friend?

What is love,
Without the fear of the Lord?
What is love,
If it's not rooted in your heart?

What is love,
Please ask yourself this question.
Love is a seed that has to grow,
To the nations, love is a true blessing!!

My Superstar

Keep me surrounded by your love,
Hold me close in your bosom, tight like a glove.
This is a love that I never felt before, every time
you touch me, I want more. The way you pour out
your love on me when I'm down,
The things you say to me when no one's around.
This is a love I cherish and can't let go,
I want to get to know you better, and our
relationship to grow. When I'm going through
trials, hold me even more tight, Watch over me,
when I sleep at night.
It's so good I can't explain the way I feel, But
deep down in my heart it's true and real. Long
as I live there's a place for you in my heart, None
other than Christ Jesus, You're my true superstar.

"I Love You"

Lord I love you more than anything,
The joy, compassion, and love that I get from you I can't explain.
You gave your son and he died for my sins, if you had to I believe you'll do it all over again. Your unconditional love, and everlasting grace and mercy, I appreciate you Lord, because you did nothing to hurt me. No one gives me greater love than you, The pain that you took for me, I don't have a clue. It had to be love, for you to die, so we can be together, you said that it would be forever. When I was sinking, you lend a helping hand, Lord Jesus, I love you, and I thank you for being a true friend!!

Love# 2

Love is a four letter word that takes a lot of action, love is pure, love hurts, sometimes it's not relaxing. Love searches the deepness of the heart, goes higher than the highest hill,

Love causes you to let go of your own will. Love is not hard to do, like nike, just do it, we will find that the flames from hell could not burn through it.

Love...... is a definition of, I'll be there when you need me, searching God's word we can hear him say just believe me!! Flesh have us searching for love in all the wrong places, have us doing things we say is love but really is outrageous. Love is something we shouldn't take for granted, because love isn't love, if it's forced and demanded... Love is a sensational feeling, so honest and sweet, something done unconditionally, that makes our whole live complete!!

Humble as a Dove

Pray for those who despitefully use you, bless those who curse you, and abuse you.

To our enemies we have to be gentle and kind, showing the love of Jesus, as we let our light shine.

First we most know that God is love, we are representatives of him, because that's whom we serve. If your enemy ask for something to drink or eat, give nicely unto him, because what you sow, unto other ye will surely reap. We have to love our enemies, as we love ourselves, Christ must be in our heart, because that's our main help. Let our main focus, be to show love, wherever we go... To be kind, gentle, and humble as a dove.

Faith

"Now faith is the substances of things hoped for
and the evidence of things not seen."
Hebrews 11:1 NKJV

Keep Hope

You are blessed, everything you touch, will prosper,

Keep looking to the hills, don't let nothing stop you.

Your friends and family holding you back, you gotta let them go, they ask you what's going on, just let them know. You have came a long ways, and you can't look back, you're going to the next level, stay on the right track. Now faith is the substance of things hope for, everything the enemy stole, will be restored. Keep on pushing, keep hope alive, you are somebody, you are the apple of God eye. Broken words will come, but let that not make you fall, be strong and of good courage, and stand tall. You are a winner no matter the weather, keep hope in Christ Jesus, in yourself, things will get better just keep hope in your eyes!!!

My Destiny

My destiny is,
To make it to the top.
Come forth as pure gold,
I can nit be stopped!!

Focusing on my dreams,
It will come to surface.
My vision is clear,
The dream-killer is worthless.

With God on my side,
I will rise!
Standing on his word,
My God will provide.

With a high level of Faith,
Failure is not what I see.
Accomplishing my dream,
For it is my... DESTINY!!!!!!

I will make it

You can make it, all you have to do is believe, tell yourself, I will not be deceived. In this life you have a purpose, don't let your self-esteem, make you feel worthless. Pick yourself up, take one step at a time, the battle that you're fighting, is all in your mind. Set a goal, and pursue after your dream. Acknowledge God, no one greater can be on your team. No matter the situation, you gotta keep your focus, that's the enemy's job to make you feel hopeless. Tell yourself, I can do all things in Christ, Jesus came and he gave us the abundance of life. When you start progressing, some people may hate it, But you keep on pushing, and tell yourself I WILL MAKE IT!!

Rejoice

Jesus Christ is the answer,
To all our problem.
Don't look to the left, don't look to the right,
Cause we can't solve them.

Wipe away your complaint,
Put trust in your maker.
Get your eyes off people,
Don't worry about the Haters!

Jesus Christ is the doorway,
To your peace and your joy.
Give everything to him,
In his name rejoice!

Help me Father

I need you,
More than you can imagine.
To uphold me,
Encourage me with compassion.

Down in my spirit,
I have no body to turn.
Uplift me heavenly father,
Don't let me cause my soul to BURN!

I need a helping hand,
But no one's there.
Who can I call on,
I've looked everywhere.

But... what is man,
He can't save my soul!
Help me my father,
Wash me, and make me as pure gold.

Hold One

No matter what your going through, hold on, when you don't know what to do, hold on.

Even when your about to give up, hold on, your heavenly father will show up if you hold on.

You don't have enough money and your bills are due, hold on, when the help from others are few, hold on.

Your money is short, no food on the table, hold on.

Keep on believing for God is able,

Problems seems like they getting harder and harder, hold on, keep striving your blessing on the border, hold on. Test and trails come to make you stronger, hold on, you're about to get a breakthrough, it want be very long, hold one. Jesus said ask, and it shall be done, Out of all you're going through, the battle's already won!! Just HOLD ON.......

VICTORY

V-means to be valiant, because we are mighty in God; he leads and guides us, and protects us with his rod.

I-means to be intelligent because we are strong and wise; and in God's eyes we're never despised.

C-means to be caring because, God is love so we must seek that love which comes from above.

T-means to be true because we have to be honest and true; God hates a liar so don't let it be you.

O-means to be obligated because we have to let go of our own will; and do the work of our father no matter how we feel.

R-means respectful, we are to recognize God as our Lord and Savior he's our creator so let's show the right kind of behavior.

Y-means to be a yielded vessel, because we will let the Holy Ghost have his way, and if you be this kind of person you will have victory each and everyday!!!

No weapon formed against me shall prosper!!

God is or fortress, our shield and our protector, no matter the situation, let God be the inspector. Greater is the man on the side of me and you, don't get weary, because he will bring you through. The enemy came to steal, kill, and destroy,

But Christ Jesus gives us the abundance of everlasting joy. Who can keep a good man down, not even Satan himself, we can conquer all things, because Christ conquered death. Our weapons are not carnal, but mighty in God, he will fight your battles even the numbers look odd.

The God we serve is great, powerful, and mighty, things we go through, to him, is small, and tiny. In our bodies, God is a miracle working doctor, He is awesome, no weapon formed against us shall prosper!!

Blessing

*"That the blessing of Abraham might come
upon the Gentiles in Christ Jesus, that we might
receive the promise of the Spirit through faith"
Galatians3:14 NKJV*

Blessing Bound

We are the head and not the tail,
The gaits of hell shall not prevail.
We are the lenders and not borrowers,
God made us true warriors.
With a cheerful heart we will give,
Made righteous through Jesus , we shall live.
Sowing seeds on holy ground,
We must know we're blessing bound!!

I'S MY SEASON

It's not over till God say it's over,

I can do all things in Christ, he made me a soldier. If God be for me, who can be against me, no one can stop the blessings, or take away what's in me. I'm more than a conqueror, keep my head held high, I can not be defeated, I got my sword and shield by my side. Christ came and he bruised the head of the snake, so called Lucifer, watch my enemies cause they fake. It's God's will for me to prosper and be blessed, I bind the spirit of poverty all it cause is stress. I have nothing to lose, but a lot to gain, keeping hope alive in Christ Jesus I shall remain. To turn my back on God I don't have a good enough reason, nothing can keep a good man down IT'S MY SEASON!!!

INHERIT THE PROMISE

God you are my provider, you are my everything, You show everlasting love when I call your name. You told me you will never leave or forsake me, You gave me power so nothing can overtake me. I thank you every day for your mercy and your grace, unconditional love shown by you, no one can take your place. I look back and see how you brought me a long way, and receive joyfully the answers from you when I pray. Lord my feelings for you are greater than before, pour out your spirit on me even greater I desire more. I thank on you and embrace, my storms shall pass, the author and finisher of my faith, how can I put you last! In Christ Jesus I am a winner, it was predestined for me to be even when I was a sinner. My eyes have not seen what God has for me, I know it's great, I am a just man not walking by sight, but by faith. Thank God for the change, at first life seemed ironic, being adopted in the kingdom of God, I shall inherit the promise!

MARRIAGE

"Marriage is honorable among all and the bed undefiled; but fornicators and adulterers God will judge." Hebrews 13:4 NKJV

MY PROMISE

I promise to love you,
I promise to always be true.
I promise to stay by your side,
No matter what we go through.

I promise not to cheat,
I promise you are my only.
I promise to hold you close,
I promise to never leave you lonely.

The words I say to you,
Are real and honest.
Vows I truly say to you,
This is my promise!!

YOUR MARRIAGE IS SWEET

Don't let nothing come between you and your spouse, tear down your marriage, or split up your house. Whatever the problem is give it unto the Lord, because if not, you'll lose someone you can't afford. The enemy will creep in through any open door, but by the grace of God your marriage will be restored. Disagreements are going to come, but you got to hold out, forgive one another, show love, speak kind words out your mouth. Don't give up just love a little more, be a friend, and learn from the mistakes you made before. In due season a change is going to come, your marriage is sweet, speak it, and it shall be done!

SPENDING TIME

We have to be willing to spend some quality time, talking and sharing to each other what's on our mind. Never put no one but God before your relationship, not mother nor father, if you do your spouse may dip. Spending time doesn't mean you have to talk the whole while, you could go riding, watch movies, cuddle up together, and smile. People got it mistaking, but time means a whole lot, don't be too busy for anyone else, or you may lose what you got. Building love through a relationship, comes through spending time, not spending time will cause someone else to be on their mind. Don't let your feelings get in the way, and cause you to be blind, cause in making a marriage strong, you got to spend some time.

MARRIAGE IS WHAT YOU MAKE IT

Hold on to your marriage, don't let go, you are to be strong, just let your love flow. Marriage can be sweet, it's what you make it, remember your spouse has a heart, so don't you break it. It's not about what you have or what you got, cause sometimes, the small things can mean a whole lot. We'll be surprised what love can do more than money, your marriage will be powerful, and sweeter than honey. Sometimes it may seem hard, and may not be easy, but gentleness plays a big part, it's peaceful and pleasing. So grab your spouse by the hand, and say how much you love each other, let your peace and love spread, your marriage will go further!

COUNT UP THE COST

Don't look at the situation you're going through right now, just trust in God and believe he'll work things out. You two can make it if you try, the love that you have for each other, don't let your problems cause it it to die. You promised to love through the good and the bad, have faith in your marriage, and believe the storm is going to past. That man you got he loves ya, that woman you got she loves ya, it's the enemy using your circumstances to turn you against each other. The love that you have built doesn't go away over night, so really, thank about the consequences, and get your mind right. Before you pack your bags you need to count up the cost, you think you won, but at the end, you'll see you have lost!

LISTEN

Be careful what you do or say, the wrong words will cause you a price you'll have to pay. Don't be too stubborn to listen to your mate, not listening can be one of your biggest mistakes. You're not a perfect person, but when your mate talks, they are trying to help you, they see some things in you, that you don't thank you do. It don't hurt to apologize, or say, baby, okay, you're showing your spouse humbleness, and you'll do anything that want push them away. In the end, you'll look back on the person you're missing, and you'll say, I wish I would've done more, but most of all, I wish I would've listened!

HUSBAND

" Husbands love your wives just as Christ also
loved the church and gave himself for her"
Ephesians 5:25 NKJV

YOUR KING

He is your Lord,
He is your king.
He's more precious than gold,
And the world's bling-bling.

God made man
In the image of himself.
To have authority over the woman,
No matter how she felt.

He is to be honored highly
Not treated like anything.
The next thing close to God,
    Wives, he is your KING!!

Last Breath

He is king of palace,
Who sits boldly on his throne.
The secret to his royalty,
To another is unknown.

He protects his beloved wife,
Who is the treasure to his heart.
Providing for the love of his life,
100% putting in his part.

He's powerful,
No one can steal his riches.
He is a man of integrity,
And a king to his mistress.

He loves his wife,
As he loves himself.
Every step of the way,
     Till he breathes his last breath.

A Queen

She is your beloved wife,
The one true, and only, love of your life.
Keep her closely knitted in your heart,
Don't let no one come in between, and split you
all apart.
Treat her nice, and with respect, cause if she
walk out of your life, that's one thing you will
regret.
    Don't get upset, just listen to her when she
talk, take time out with her, even if it's, a nice
long walk.
Give her a hot bath, message her feet when they
hurt, to keep this special woman, you have to put
in some work.
Say nice things to her, make your woman smile,
she will give you something back that will make
you go WILD!! When she's down, encourage her,
and give nice things, cherish the one your with
and treat her like a queen

Wife

"The wise woman builds her house. But the foolish pulls it down with her hands" Proverbs 14:1 NJKV

Apple of my Eye

She is intelligent, and she is wise,
   She is the glory of a man, and the apple of his eyes.
   God made woman, to be beautiful creatures, special to a man and has spectacular features. She is to be loved and held, embraced closely when needed, soft words whispered in her ear and nicely treated.
   Her beauty is to catch her husband's attention, she is attractive to him, daily to her, that should be mentioned.
   Enjoy your wife in the time of your youth, respect her will and mind, always be honest and true. Because you don't miss your well, till your water runs dry, So love her unconditionally, and remember she's the apple of your eye!!

My Wife

She is flesh of my flesh, bone of my bone,
Someone I love dearly, and can't leave alone.
She is my joy, and the apple of my eye.
Comfort and hold her, when she weep and cry.
A beautiful woman that's so tender and sweet,
what will I be without her, she make my life
complete.
Whatever I need, she's there by my side,
With her alone, I'm happy and Satisfied. Her
beauty shines off the glow of her skin, she gives
me love, that lies within.
To sum it all down she is the love of my life,
someone beautiful and special, I call her my
wife!!

Making love all night

She is one of a kind,
   Another woman like her, is impossible to find.
   She is a pot of gold, and man's treasure, a
touch so soft lighter than a feather. A brilliant
mind, with and intelligent figure, The love
given by her make you skin shiver.
   Another woman can't compare to the things
that she do,
   When she a lot of love to give and she give
it all to you. She know the things to do that
brightens up your day, doing things to drive
you wild, having you wordless with nothing to
say. A woman like this, I love to love her right,
holding her, kissing her, making love all night.

SHE LIGHTS UP MY DAY

Where would I be without you, the woman whom I enjoy in the time of my youth. It makes me happy just to see your face, and the smile you give lights up the whole place. You are someone special and adorable to my sight, to see you happy and peaceful is what I like. A wonderful person is what you are to me, an angel on this earth, and a jewel is what I see. My love for you, baby, it flows like a river, I picture your face in my mind like it reflects through a mirror. The woman that I have is a precious human being, more valuable than riches, she is an adorable queen. She is more than what words can explain or say, she is like the sun, that sits high in the sky, and she lights up my day.

MY WIFE

It's our wedding day, and she's looking so marvelous, like the presence of a queen, I'm astonished by her royalness. As she comes down the isle, she floats like a butterfly, happiness fills my heart, I'm astonished by my eyes. As I see the woman of my dreams coming down the isle, I'm heated on the inside by the apperance of a beautiful smile. I've never seen anything more beautiful in my life, than the woman I see today that's about to be my wife. She looks like an angel sitting high in the sky, kissing her softly, is how I want to reply. Can't fight this feeling, no matter how hard I try, one thing I know, she'll make one beautiful wife!

FAMILY

" I will bless those who bless you, and curse him who curse you; and in you all the families of the earth shall be blessed." Genesis 12:3 NKJV

HAPPY FAMILY

We all are sisters and brothers,
We all bleed the same blood no matter our
colors.
We serve the same God, we breathe the same
air, we are all human beings, kept under God's
perfect care.
We aren't all the same, we come in different
shapes, and different sizes,
We are all God's creation, when are we going to
realize it?
So let's not hate each other and become our own
enemy,
Let's show the love of Jesus, and become one big
happy family!

FAMILY

We will be united, we will stick together,
No matter the storm, we will survive the weather.
You need me and I need you,
To handle the trials that we must go through.
When you're down they're there to pick you up,
Giving good words of encouragement, when
times looking rough.
At times we do things each of us don't
understand,
But one thing about family, they're there to lend
a helping hand.
No matter near or far, family will always be
close,
People who is always kept in the heart, dearly
cherished the most!

FAMILY TREE

We are all brothers and sisters,
We must understand.
Why hate one another,
That's not our father's plan.

What will it profit us,
To cause the knife to fit in our back.
It's solves nothing,
There's no profit in that.

Different sizes, different shapes,
Different forms and fashions.
We still need one another,
We never know what can happen.

I need you,
And you need me.
So let's let our lives grow,
As one Christian family tree!!

FAMILY

Having a family is adorable, sharing life with the woman of your kids is joyful. Watching your kids get bigger, day by day, laughing at some of the silly things they say. Holidays roll around, we prepare for a family feast. Looking from past to present, of the goals we have reached. Oh, how good it feels to be around your loved ones. Enjoying the most wonderful times of your lives under the sun. We should thank God, for this blessing and this favor, giving us a family, to enjoy and love, life doesn't get any greater!